I'M NOT OK!

W.T.F do I do NOW?

The book that changes you AS you read it!

MAZ SCHIRMER

Copyright © 2018
Maz Schirmer

All rights reserved. This book is copyright. Apart from any use as permitted under the Copyright Act 1968 no part of this publication may be reproduced, stored in a retrieval system or transmitted in any form or by any means, electronic, mechanical, photocopying, recording or otherwise, without the prior consent of the copyright holder.

The moral right of the author has been asserted.

The information contained in this book is intended to be for educational purposes only and is not intended for diagnosis, treatment, or prescription of any health related disorder whatsoever. The information contained in this book should not replace consultation with a relevant medical or healthcare professional. The author and publisher are in no way liable for any incorrect interpretation or misuse of the information contained herein.

ISBN: 978-0-6483545-0-5

SPECIAL NOTE

This book is NOT written in a grammatically correct manner on PURpose. It's written in a uNIQUE and POWERful way that's been designed to transFORM your mind WHILE you read and learn. It's NOT hypnosis or anything like that. It's introducing the information in the book to your brain in STEREO rather than mono for a more IMpacting result.

Be sure to EMphasise the words or syllables that are in CAPITALS only. Read it with PASSION in your voice as IF you're narrating it to someone ELSE, someone you REALLy want to help.

You get to be your own coach AND the student at the SAME time!

DEDICATION

To the resilience of the human spirit
and our ability to RISE ABOVE it!

THANK YOU

All proceeds from the original sale
of this book goes to the RISE ABOVE
IT Charity to support preventative
programs and provide practical
resources for all ages with the aim of
breaking the cycle.

ABOUT THE AUTHOR

As The Author I (and everyone who EVER changed their life and dug their way out of their rut) was triggered with FIRST deciding

"MY LIFE IS W.T.F (**W**orth **T**he **F**ight)"

I personally broke free from a 30 year cycle of doom created from my own past of poverty, domestic violence and sexual abuse both as a child and adult.

My first suicide attempt was at 8 years old.

After my W.T.F moment I entirely broke my cycle and discovered I wasn't dumb and useless after all, in fact I released a creativity within me that would have never been discovered.

I've gone from an unemployed waitress,

single mum of 4 who lived in hiding for more than a year, riddled with fears and insecurities, with ZERO confidence who couldn't even eye contact people, believing I was LESS valuable than the chewing gum on someone's shoe, to becoming the designer of a new style of therapies with therapists practicing in 11 countries to date, setting everyday peoples hearts free.

I'm now an Amazon best-selling author of multiple books, international award-winning innovator and the pioneer of revolutionary breakthrough tools and resources that have transformed thousands of lives. I am also featuring my unique mind-resetting tools in a Hollywood full featured movie called IMPACT. W.T.F (Worth The Fight)? You bet!

Who'd have thought a little downtrodden Aussie girl from a tiny beach community called Flying Fish Point who'd all but given up would one day receive a call from a Hollywood documentary movie director?

ANYTHING is possible for ANYONE when they understand what I've simplified in layman's terms within this short little book.

I TOO thought my life was impossible to change, once, BUT it all starts with a deCISION and I want YOU to know the TRUTH about what it REALLY takes so you TOO can rise above it, activate your creative and potential and GET ON WITH IT!

- There IS hope
- You CAN rise above it
- You CAN feel different about yourself, others AND your life
- You CAN regain control of your life
- There IS a solution (in your hand right now)
- You HAVEN'T tried everything
- You AREN'T alone, even if you think you are
- People CHANGE everyDAY, they really DO
- It's NOT your 'lot' in life
- You AREN'T meant to suffer
- You're NOT too old
- You ARE loveable
- You ARE strong enough
- You ARE smart enough

- You ARE worthy
- You ARE deserving
- YOU. ARE. ENOUGH
- You CAN change
- You AREN'T too far gone
- Your life is AS valuable as ANYone else's
- NO one can help you if you don't ALSO help yourself
- No one owes you ANYTHING
- It's NEVER too late
- You deSERVE to be fully heard and not judged
- There IS choice, even if you can't see it yet

(Print off a copy of these ATTITUDE ADJUSTMENT pages and read often)

I'm Not OK

It's OK that you're NOT ok!

Sometimes it's sunny, sometimes it drizzles with rain, sometimes it BUCKETS down, and every now and then we must bunker down for a category 5 and hang on for dear life!

Whatever it is that's going on for you right now and how ever long it's been going on, you're allowed to FEEL what you FEEL. The good, the bad and the ugly, because you may be surprised to learn that many other human beings probably feel, or have felt, like YOU do right now. It's TRUE.

It's NORMal to go through stages of your life, even looooong stages, where you feel like crap or like giving up. We can all become overwhelmed with stress, depression and anxiety, to the point of hopelessness, but it's STAYING there that's the real problem. WHAT can you do about it?

DECIDE YOU ARE Worth The Fight!

GET AN ATTITUDE! FIGHT your way back! ONLY. YOU. Can DO that!

Giving up is EASY because it appears to be the less painful option BUT that's SHORT term thinking and the one thing that we are ALL individually gifted with, is TIME. Thank goodness for that I hear you say ;)

You've survived everything else, haven't you? If you've never been through what you're going through now, someone ELSE has and THEY made it through. In fact MANY others have, reGARDless of what IT is.

YOU CAN TOO!

You CAN survive this and you can EVEN THRIVE. It's TRUE!

You MUST, at a time of crisis, seek out HOPE and HELP but eVENtually it's YOU who will have to help yourSELF.

SEEK to follow and hang with people who will supPORT you and ALLOW you to process what's happened because this is the START of getting through ANYthing. Read inSPIRING triUMPHant stories of others who endured and lived through what YOU'RE going through. Do it!!!

The MORE you feel like NOT doing it, the MORE you HAVE TO do it.

We've compiled some such stories into the back of this book where people, ORDINARY Aussies, ROSE ABOVE IT, AGAINST THE ODDS and looking back are SO **VERY** glad they DIDN'T give up.

They deCIDED they were **W**orth **T**he **F**ight then fought for their lives and WON. Let that be YOU!

It's YOUR job to take that first step and it's REALLY hard at times to get up off the ground, but step by step and one bite at a time, you can EVEN eat an elephant... but don't. Poor elephant! ;)

Watch funny movies, make yourself laugh. Go find some kids to play with because maybe you're being a boring old teen or stuffy old adult who's been 'adulting' for TOOOOOOOO long being TOOOOOOOO serious.

It's been scientifically proven that when you feel like crap on the inside the mere act of FORCING a smile can CHANGE your MOOD. Sounds too simple but hey, what do you have to lose? Lots right! So give it a go! NOW! Smile.........;) See, now HOLD that smile regardless of your thoughts. Longer... hold it for 5 minutes. Set a timer on your mobile RIGHT NOW! Let this be your VERY. FIRST step to PROVE you CAN do something for your OWN well-being.

FORCE it and HOLD it for the full 5 minutes then congratulate yourself. Each time you fight your gloom pattern you send a message to your UNconscious mind that you WANT to change, that you WANT to behave differently.

MOVE, MOVE, MOVE that body of yours. Stillness, without the objective of seeking solution is only going to create a HOLDING pattern and eVENTually you'll run out of fuel and crash.

Don't be alone for too long at any time either. Even if it's the LAST thing you WANT to do, go find people and be NEAR them. Inter-ACT (take actions involving others) !!!

You may never be quite the same if

you've lost someone precious to you, and by no means do you have to forget them, but one thing's fairly universal, in that the person who's no longer walking this earth with you would WANT you to be happy.

In FACT the loss of your loved one could FUEL you to make the MOST of your life by dedicating it to them, seeing as they no longer have the opportunity.

If you're still grieving and unable to yet move on, then REvisit this book later and keep it in a safe place until you ARE ready to feel better.

THAT'S OK!

There is NO right or wrong way to grieve. If anyone tells you you're 'supPOSed to' grieve for 'x' length of time, ask them how they know that to be true. There are many rules in society that lead to misery, anxiety and depression that are just fallacies made up by some human in times gone by. These fallacies have become the rules yet are rooted in fear and the belief that suffering is somehow noble.

If someone tells you there IS a timeframe or puts any guilt trips on you, remember, you are YOU and they are THEM and GUILT is the most USEless of ALL human emotions because we think it's a moral compass... but it's NOT. The premise of guilt is that you are not good enough as you are so you NEED rules to be good. You're as good as a tree is. You ARE nature.

YOU have a HEART and you're GOOD with or without a compass.

YOU, yes YOU, are alREADY INNATELY GOOD, with or withOUT your belief system. Right and wrong have been SOLD to us by institutions set up by HUMAN beings just like you and me who wanted to control people, however many of these beliefs are not mind and heart healthy.

They are built on the foundation of FEAR and stop us from ever feeling GOOD enough or WHOLE and comPLETE. No WONDER we're confused and don't know how to just 'BE' anymore.

Living this way, fearing we are evil if we don't 'should' all over the place, eventually leads to anxiety, stress and panic because we're not living true to OURselves, but rather to OTHER people's expectations FROM and OF us.

Most GOALS lead to us feeling WORSE because we fail by procrastinating, due to not TRULY being in alignment with what WE want, but rather we are led by the PRESSure of feeling the need to please a society or aNOTHER person such as a parent, or even our own EGO which is based on OTHER people's approval.

These are OTHER people's rules and values, cast ON to us. This life is YOURS and as long as you don't hurt anyone ELSE, you can make your OWN rules of how to 'be' YOU.

Are you living true to YOUR OWN set of standards and PERSONAL desires?

Yes, yes, of course rules of the road and surviving in a community are essential for safety BUT if the rules are about how you should 'FEEL' or 'BE' that causes you stress or misery, then ask your 'GUT' if they serve your own ultimate peace, happiness and higher GOOD.

Ask yourself, "Am I trying to conform to please OTHERS at the COST of my OWN happiness?" because sometimes there's nothing wrong with you, except you're hanging with people who care more about THEIR rules and values than YOUR happiness.

Perhaps you need to have a

conversation or create boundaries? The AVOIDANCE of tackling a situation that needs addressing will only lead to long-term depression or resentment.

There is ALways a group you can find who think like YOU do and 'BE' like YOU want to BE, who don't harm others in the process and don't lay guilt trips on YOU for being YOU. Go find THOSE people. THEY are YOUR people.

Your uNIQUE self is 100% YOURS. Be sure you're leaving YOUR uNIQUE footprint on this planet and you CAN do it how YOU want to do it. Remember who YOU are and what YOU want and need to feel GOOD again.

If you've lost someone to suicide, that's really tough.

As hard as it is to understand this, it was THEIR decision and reGARDless of how it went down, you did NOT CAUSE it because THAT choice could only be made by them, even if it's the only choice THEY could see at the time, they did in fact have another choice available, and that was to NOT take their life. Someone different may have chosen a DIFFerent reaction if it was central around something that happened between you.

We are each responsible for our OWN behaviours and choices. To blame others is to NOT take our own responsibility for it.

Self-blame is FRUITless and only leads to feelings of helplessness and hopelessness. This self-punishment will end up creating needless stress and internal pain. DON'T do that! LEARNing from events is what's meant to happen from them, not degrading yourself because of them.

Have you heard the saying that resentment (towards others or yourself) is like drinking poison but expecting the other person to suffer?

You can't undo what's happened or bring them back, but YOU are still alive. Ensure YOU make MORE of your opportunity to live and breathe, to walk and talk, to love and feel, to learn and grow, to experience through all 5 or more senses and express it fully. You VALUE yours MORE than they did. LEARN from it. Let it make you BETTer NOT bitter or obsessed in their memory.

What if you DO have a creator; what would THEY want you to do? Hate yourself, or forgive yourself and just NEVER do it again? Most likely.

Be gentle to the child you once were because he or she did NOT die!

Look in the mirror for you ARE her or him. NOTHING'S changed other than events and time. What if time never existed? You're still you! YOU are the sweet innocent fun adventurous child you were born to be. Re-connect to your inner child. You are NOT separate from him or her.

Don't say ANYTHING to yourself that you wouldn't say to a small innocent child.

If that child were to come back at that same age and you got to meet him or her, what does he or she need MOST that he or she isn't getting, because it is YOU who is the gate-keeper of love. If you can't find value or unconditional acceptance and love in your child-self, no-one else can because as the gate-keeper you'll block it from getting through.

LOVE STARTS WITH YOU LOVING YOURSELF!

YOU get up and FIGHT for LOVE!

It's YOUR fight because it's YOUR life so it's up to YOU to FIGHT for it whether you're aLONE or you have support!

Other people can only help by inspiring something in YOU and we often mistakenly give them OUR power, thinking they SHOULD be able to do more FOR us, but that's not how things work.

Without your commitment to getting happy, they CAN'T help you, even if they want to. You've GOT to show up, not just physically but in reSOLVE to moving forward.

It's also hard for someone to know exACTly what to do to help you, because they are NOT YOU.

Everyone is SO unique and, when it comes to matters of the mind and heart, it's not like fixing a broken teapot. At the end of the day, any advice — even the BEST ADVICE ON THE PLANET — is not going to help you if you've already given up.

So get an attitude of W.T.F.

Because YOU are **W**ORTH **T**HE **F**IGHT!

Edwin Louis Cole once said, *"You don't drown by FALLing in the water; you drown by STAYING there."*

RISE to the challenge of fighting for a BETTER life because no one ELSE is going to do it for you!

Get an ATTITUDE of GRATITUDE for the GIFT of YOUR life, the one YOU were given and reCLAIM it and reCREATE it, if need be. Some people have never HAD the opportunity. Milk it for what you can GET from this life of YOURS.

NO it's NOT easy but...

YOU. CAN. DO. IT!

It's your birthright to be happy, content and feel joy...even if you can't see that now!

We live ONE life only (that we know of for sure) and you get ONE chance at it, so don't waste any more time needlessly suffering. Take ACTION. Take action HERE and NOW!

NO-one has more to lose or should be AS inVESTed in the quality of YOUR life than YOU. Simply put, you won't get to feel in control of your life UNTIL you take YOUR life into your OWN hands.

Don't get lulled into the false sense of COMfort that sympathy or avoidance brings. It's UNHEALTHy on ALL levels and eats away at your spirit until the force of life is so sucked out of you, even your breath becomes shallow.

Life is literally sucking out of you and you end up leTHARgic and TIRED and exHAUSTed and yet you haven't DONE anything to justify feeling so wrecked and worn.

You have to get UP for yourSELF, and THEN seek the kind of help from someone (friend or counsellor) you're WILLing to, not just be SAVED by, but PARTner UP with and inVEST yourself wholeheartedly into. THIS is the ONLY way FORward.

That could be THIS book, a person or a program or ANY support. Seek help in a pro-ACTIVE manner, honouring YOUR part in the PARTnership.

People WANT to help people who are helping themselves and can only REALLY help those people ANYway. The fight is NOT against others, it's against GIVING UP.

Where's your fighting spirit?!

Some things are WORTH fighting for and YOU my friend are ONE of them!

It's OK to be VULNERAble. In fact, it's the STRONGest thing you'll ever do.

If you've been a victim in the TRUE sense of the word (something outside of your control happened TO you) — esPECIALly if it involves an unresolved injustice (done by you or someone else TO you) — you may not have been able to move on from the past.

If you feel there is no-one in your life presently that you can turn to SEE OUR

SUGGESTED HELPLINE SUPPORT SERVICES ON PAGE 128.

Maybe you've not yet been FULLY heard in a NON-judgemental way by a comPASSIONATE person?

Opening up, ignites HEALing so you can move FORward. It's WORTH seeking someone trustworthy and compassionate to hear you out comPLETEly, IF you feel you need to, but do it for the PURPOSE of getting it OUT because it's HEALTHy, NOT for the purpose of sympathy or being doted on.

You might have shared your story but to the wrong people or under the wrong circumstances, but there's MORE people, there's MORE solutions; you just have to FIND them because THEY are NOT searching for YOU.

CAUTION: as healthy and healing as talking CAN be, the flip side of the coin is, the MORE times you tell your story, the MORE you ingrain it and eVENTually you end up feeling so sorry for yourSELF that you feel helpless and hopeless and the ONLY time you feel in control is when you're telling it AGAIN which is not really control at all, it's an unhealthy addiction to sympathy which will keep you in the cycle you want to break free from.

Yes, it's left you scarred and you can't undo the past and it's NOT FAIR, BUT you CAN stop it dictating your future.

Fight for a BETTER future that's NOT based on the past.

What happens TO you is NOT WHO you ARE because you're WAYYYYYYYYY more than that.

When you see yourself as being here for a purpose you step into your LEADer self. You need to do that now and LEAD your way out.

The usual process of fixing our problem is to go to an expert, but often their focus is on diagnosing, understanding or BANDaiding, not teaching YOU to DRIVE yourSELF in a way that aVOIDS the crash and burn in the FIRST place.

They top up the fuel tank (we need that too) but don't TEACH you how to top it up YOURself so you don't keep breaking down in the FIRST place.

We easily value investing our time into learning enough about driving and maintaining a car to at least be able to get from A to B and AVOID breaking down along the way, but we don't learn to drive OUR OWN SELF.

Do you get a mechanic to teach you to drive? NO, you don't need to know the ins and outs of HOW the engine under the hood works just to DRIVE the machine. You don't have to become a psychologist to be able to DRIVE your own mind.

Sadly, we know more about how to maneuver and maintain a car than how to drive our own mind, like this book is teaching you to do, alREADY.

We value investing time and effort into our physical health but is our mind (conscious and unconscious) not the entire instructor of all our organs, including our brain?!

Your mind runs your body and all its parts — ALL of them — your moods, your monthly cycle (if you're female), and even knows your conditioned and inherited patterns of behaviours and all of your likes, dislikes and your secrets. It makes your decisions — the good the bad and the ugly — and does EVERYthing it's been programmed to do... programmed BY YOU, intentionally or not!

The sum total of how you see yourself, others and THE ENTIRE WORLD is programming (a record on replay learning occasional new information) because reGARDless of whether you believe that or not, SOMEone SOMEwhere in the world has an entirely POLAR OPPOSITE belief and THEY justify THEIR belief the same way you do YOURS.

Who's got the secret to happiness? Is it the giggling, smiling African woman I saw in Zimbabwe, walking along a bush track with her children on her way home to her mud hut miles from the UNICEF water pump where the ONLY drinkable water was?

Atop her head was a ten gallon bucket of water, a baby on her front in a wrap and a small toddler walking barefoot beside her over the harsh dried clay.

We arrived at the hut to be told that very woman had to put her baby to sleep each night in a net flung from the roof so it wouldn't be taken and eaten by lions while she slept, like OTHER babies in their tribe had been.

OR...

Is it someone you THINK is happier because they have what you DON'T have and are DOING what YOU want to be doing?

What if it's NOT hard at ALL to shift your thinking to support where YOU want to go? What if it matters NOT what your IQ or bank account reflects or whether you've found your ideal partner? There are MANY happy people who LOVE their own company and doing WHAT they want WHEN they want regardless of a partner in life.

Ok, I hear you, that's not what YOU want but can you see that perSPECTive truly can be ALL you need to work on to turn your life around? THEN you can work on the rest of your life and it can EVEN be enJOYable. YES IT **IS** POSSIBLE!

As you're reading this, notice your THOUGHTS... The MORE they're doubting the MORE you need to tell those thoughts to shut up because THAT'S sabotage. Up until now, you've ALLOWED these thoughts by not challenging them.

Your thoughts are just the same old regurgitated sabotaging argument most of the time anyway, all 50,000+ of them.

Knowing HOW to CHANGE these patterns, to FREEZE the circuitry, interRUPT the software long enough for you to get a fresh perspective, is what happens when you do the snappy little processes we've included in this book.

We wanted to give you something YOU can do for YOURself, without having to get a degree in psychology just to learn the minimal basics of how to drive yourself;

You can begin to TRAIN your mind, without too much effort throughout a busy day. It's about re-dirECTing your mind when something takes you off course.

The mindset-adjusting tools in this book are for YOU to be able to reCALibrate your OWN emotions, so you can LEARN from your life situations to choose the BEST perspective for YOU and YOUR inner peace and happiness.

These tools are for LIFE, so whenever you need to pick yourSELF up in the future you will have these strategies at hand.

BUT FIRST...

When you imagine you see a snake crossing your path on a lovely moonlit evening, and it turns out to be just a stick, for a moment in time your body releases the EXACT SAME blend of stress chemicals into your bloodstream and even prickles your skin over your enTIRE body.

That means, iMAGINed reality can be JUST as powerful as reALITY itself. That's HOW powerful YOUR MIND is and YOU'RE driving this ship, believe it or not!

It's time to become aware of yourself OR you can continue to wing it but if nothing changes nothing changes.

Your mind CAN change and that's the most important message of the times. There IS hope!

Our mind is NOT a big monster to be feared; it's there to HELP us. It's a Genie in a bottle and we just need to learn HOW to RUB it. When you DRIVE your OWN mind to think differently, you'll FEEL better about EVERYTHING!

Just like a car can be used to run someone over, it can ALSO be used as an ambulance to save a life. A pool can be enjoyed for playful summer fun or you can drown in it. Your brain can create fear or peace, anxiety or calm. It's how it's being used.

Events are interpreted by YOU and YOUR mind, and the interpreTATION that we EACH apply to events is what we CAN change and, in fact, ARE changing, RIGHT here, RIGHT now.

Yes this book is a bunch of repeated messages but you NEED that. The brain only picks up one-fifth of what it sees or hears so anything retained would have to be repeated at least five times so KEEP READING REGARDLESS. Let this sink in.

You'll find these tools are taught in layman terms and are so easy to use you can EVEN teach kids to use them.

It's time to learn how to navigate your emotional and mental reality from where it is, to a better place....

But FIRST, you must understand you are NOT ALONE! Others walked this walk yet turned their life around reGARDless.

Here's just 5 of the millions who have done what YOU are about to do.....

STEP 1:
DECIDE YOU ARE W.T.F! (WORTH THE FIGHT!)

Kylie, Paul H, Hannah, Jaimie and Paul S did! Luckily!

Which one do YOU relate to most?

KYLIE

Kylie was born into a family of mental health issues and abuse. She lost several of her close family members to suicide and struggled for twenty years with her own mental health. Kylie is now a HAPPY married mum, with two of her four kids with special needs and one in a wheelchair. You can read Kylie's story on page 97.

True Stories

PAUL H.

Paul H was a policeman, husband and father. He thought he had it all until suddenly, without warning, his wife left him for another man. In the process he also lost his relationship with his kids. Paul is now HAPPILY roaming the South QLD hinterlands on his BMW motorcycle and has reconnected with his children and grandchildren. You can read Paul's story on page 104.

HANNAH

Hannah, from as young as age 12, was self-harming. She was hospitalised with a severe eating disorder and wanted to die before she turned 21. Hannah is now fully recovered, engaged to be married and LIVING her life by giving back. You can read Hannah's story on page 110.

JAIMIE

Jaimie was a happy go lucky kid until the age of twelve when her dad suffered a cardiac arrest in front of her. The following three and a half years saw her stuck in a cycle of persistent PTSD (Post Traumatic Stress Disorder) afraid of anything and everything. Jaimie has now fully recovered and is pursuing her dream of becoming a professional dancer and is LIVING life to the fullest. You can read Jaimie's story on page 115.

PAUL S.

Paul S was a young man in his early twenties who on the outside looked like he had it all. A great job in construction, a loving wife and kids... but he also had a secret drug habit and alcohol addiction. His volatile relationship disintegrated, a bitter custody battle followed and Paul found himself divorced and alone. Paul has since rebuilt his life and changed direction in his career to bring HOPE to other men. You can read Paul's story on page 121.

Now that you know a little bit about each person and THEIR story, it's imPORTant to CHOOSE ONE of them to read beFORE CONTINUING ON to the next section of this book.

This will be your FUEL for later. Follow the process as instructed for the best result from this transformational handbook, EVEN if you've read a thousand books before.

Go NOW and read the story you have chosen... BE inSPIREd!

IMPORTANT: Do NOT continue on UNLESS you have read ONE of the stories. If you haven't, go NOW and read ONE of these stories first. If you have, GREAT! Let's keep going...

> "Words (including thoughts) are the containers for power.
>
> You choose what kind of power they carry."
>
> [Joyce Meyer]

We can SOMEtimes be aFRAID of changing because we fear we may LOSE a part of ourselves and NObody wants that; we're helping YOU to simply SHINE your brightest, BE your best and DO your best, as YOU.

Let's take the time to understand the bare bones minimum of how to tune our OWN engine and fuel our OWN mind, so we can help ourSELVES to RISE aBOVE life's curve-balls. Because one thing's guaranteed, and that is that

SH!T HAPPENS!

Our feelings, beliefs, thoughts and perceptions are not WHO we are, because like you witnessed with Kylie, the two Pauls, Hannah and Jaimie, they feel MORE at home in who they are NOW because they're more at peace INside.

It's very empowering to feel in control of your life.

We've always thought our CURRENT behaviours and reactions were being ingrained due to the accumulated experiences we've had since we were kiddlywinks and YES this is PART of what makes us behave as we do, BUT we've ALL witnessed the opposite too, where the most loved child grows up to be a murderer and the underdog deFIES this rule having been UNaffected by a tragic childhood or past.

HowEVER... drumroll here because this next part is revolUTIONary and SHOULD be FRONT page of EVERY newspaper because it makes SO. MUCH. SENSE. Maybe not at first but play along OK. Are you ready?

What if YOUR issue is NOT even of YOUR lifetime but the deep intrinsic root CAUSE fuelling your overall perception choices from your ancestors handed down to you through your DNA, still playing out as instructions on how to be YOU? YOU are an individual yes but ALSO you're a version of THEM (your ancestors), being experienced NOW.

This science is called Epigenetics. In layman's terms, they've discovered we CAN inherit mental and emotional issues as WELL as our nanas knobby knees, mums green eyes and dads receding hair line.

Traumatic behavioural triggers and responses can be passed down through generations too, especially where something was unexpectedly shocking such as a famine or great loss.

In OTHER words YOUR intense anxiety may have been 'paid forward' TO you from your ancestors who wore YOUR genes beFORE they got to YOU and may have experienced a heinous and shocking event.

So, by CHANGing how WE view our self, people, events and the world at large, we LITERALLY change the direction of our destiny.

This re-assigning of 'meaning', is what breaks the CYCLE rather than learning to 'cope' with the symptom forever more which let's face it folks, many of us tried this for years and it can be tiring.

It's not just about YOU, you're one of the 'now living' persons of an ancestral bloodline, the symptom if you will, not the CAUSE.

Stay with me... It's not as kooky as it sounds, you can google all about this AFTER you read this book.

Epigenetics brings the BIGGEST HOPE in the mental health and personal development industries ON. THE. PLANET.

Put simply, it means we CAN change OUR behaviours and attitudes through changing the MEANing around the behavioural triggers, organically, rather than by band-aiding. It's NOT hopeless ANY. MORE!

You're NOT destined for a future based

on your ancestor's sufferings. You CAN break the cycle and even creATE a NEW, imPROVED story and pass THAT one on to your kids.

You see, you must keep the SAME belief system as your ancestors with the SAME responses to similar triggers and events to keep the destined pattern running. Change THEM and YOU get to be that one who breaks the chain and is set FREE of your ancestral curse.

We've become accustomed to giving our POWER away by seeking help with our emotional and mental issues (a bunch of thoughts and feelings) from EXperts.

How can anyone OTHER than your OWN unconscious mind know how, why or what YOUR ancestors experienced? Are we expecting the impossible from experts?

So how can OTHER people fix OUR

unique self when we're playing out a predisposed behaviour that didn't even originate from our lifetime? If you DON'T change your perspective, you're up against willpower or having to numb your feelings and responses by consuming mind-altering 'substances' (drugs and addictive substances) and it can feel tiresome and hopeless and lead to OTHER problems.

It can all sound pie in-the-sky sci-fi but it's a part of our very NATure that science had missed for the previous 50 years believing we were doomed if it was in our genes.

OTHER people can HELP and TEACH us to SEE our current choices and perceptions to deCIDE to make BETTER choices and endlessly rely on inconsistent WILLpower, however techniques like I'm sharing with you in this book will creATE the DEEPER change, thus breaking the cycle.

CHANGing our thoughts and perceptions is the FASTEST, SIMPLEST route to changing our life because our reALity begins on the INside.

Our ability to be in control of our minds health is in our OWN hands; MORE than we've been led to believe! HALLELUJAH because with TOOLS like we've put together here for you, you CAN drive your mind conSTRUCTively.

ENDless sessions of TALK therapy with a professional where you have to re-live your story again and again is NO longer the ONLY help available.

YOU ARE the one with the POWer! So CLAIM it!

Even if you've been a victim of circumstance, YOU are the one who controls its effect on you from THIS. MOMENT. FORWARD.

This book isn't about justice or fairness, because let's face it sometimes bad stuff happens to good people and life's not fair at all. Sometimes justice will not be served and we can't do a damn thing about it [Stomp fist on table] BUT you aren't doomed to the almighty grudge with a life sentence, even though it can feel like you have no choice.

What you CAN focus on is YOU, because reGARDless of what is happening TO you, it's YOUR RESPONSES and perception (what stuff means, according to you) that causes the suffering WITHIN you. In no way does saying that, condone the behaviours of people or circumstance though.

All that REAlly matters is your HAPPYness RIGHT here and RIGHT now, because that's the ONly thing in life that NO one else can make you feel.

You CAN change, regardless of whether you have gone to counsellor after counsellor, therapist after therapist. Even if you're STILL stuck years later; because here's the thing:

"The teacher arrives ONLY when the student's ready."

That means we can only REALLY receive the message when we are READY for that message. Readiness is important! Maybe NOW IS the RIGHT time...

You must be READY to change, NOT just WANT to change.

Are you READY?

Timing matters because of the follow-through required to make the perceived life adjustments. Because we KNOW that WE are the one who will be responsible (without any more excuses) to get off our butts and TAKE that action we continually avoid or are afraid to. If we foresee it'll have to get worse before it'll get better, we'll SABOtage ourselves. We avoid pain and move towards pleasure, even if the pleasure is just slightly less pain than the painful option.

We'd RAther choose the 'comfortably familiar' than the 'UNcomfortably UNfamiliar'.

There are absolutely, DEFINITEly, changes that have to be made BY YOU in your exTERNal environment when making changes INternally. BIG DEAL! Focus on LONG term for a change! We are often wanting to opt out of life when we feel trapped in the NOW or PAST horrible moments, not trusting that we've survived things before and OTHER people have survived much worse.

It's important you shift your FOCUS to be on what you DO want, because when you're stuck in life, you become very much focused on the PROBlem and NOT the solUtion. It's NATural by the way but it's ALSO natural for SOME people to be MORE focused on the positives in life, (especially with the right mindset-altering tools), and they are the MOST resilient people of all.

Are YOU ready to become RESILIENT?!

You must be willing to own your OWN role in your life.

For example, have you ever found yourself in a relationship that failed because of the other person's behaviours? When in hindsight, if you were to be brutally honest with yourself, at some point when you first met them you made a CHOICE to continue the relationship when your gut INSTINCT told you not to.

IF you'd CHOSEN to follow your gut instinct you would NOT have experienced the pain — physically, mentally or emotionally — that followed. You may have been a victim in the true sense of the word while you had no control THEN, but you can RECLAIM it now, from this point forward.

Blame blocks any chance of feeling empowered, whether they are literally to blame, or not. It keeps you stuck in the cycle of feeling helpless and hopeless.

You think it's just ONE issue when it's a cycle.

It's time to declare WAR!!! War on GIVING UP! Delete it from your options!

Commit to changing your life for the better with the SAME level of conviction presidents of countries use when THEY declare war! NO MORE! You are the president of 'ME Incorporated' and you want peace and are WILLing to make whatever choices are necessary to make that happen.

It's time to make a commitment, in STONE;

STEP 2:
START TAKING ACTION
(EVEN IF THEY ONLY SEEM LIKE BABY STEPS)

I hereby Pledge;

"To honour and obey, for better or for worse, for richer or for poorer, in sickness and in health, till death do us part, from this day forward, my decision to give myself a check-up from the neck-up and focus on what I CAN do. It's time to move forward and break this cycle because

I AM

Worth

The

Fight!"

Signed:

....

Date: .... / .... / ....

Have you ever driven somewhere and can't remember the journey? For example you can't remember how you made it to your destination safely because you were zoned out or your mind was distracted? So what PART of you was driving the car and had you arrive SAFEly?

The part that drives US to do what we do, is the same part of us that drives our car when we're busily thinking and feeling. This is often referred to as the UNconscious mind so that's what we'll call it in this book. It's the REAL driver of you.

Your UNconscious mind RUNS your LEARNED and inHERITED cycles, beliefs and behaviours on automation (reGARDless of where they came from). This ALL happens OUTSIDE of your awareness, day in day out, second by second, so YOU can get on with learning OTHER things — or in THIS case, we want to use it to UNlearn sabotaging patterns and replace them with a BETTER program, one WE choose on PURpose. ;)

The part we often refer to as our brain, (which we've been taught to value so highly) where we make decisions etc. and houses our so called 'intelligence' we'll call the CONscious mind.

It's the part of us that likes to THINK it's in control, but it's been given too much credit. Most people try to change by ONLY working at this level and they fail because they don't factor in the 'automation' part, which is the UNconscious mind always running in the BACKground.

YES the Conscious mind is the instructor, but it's NOT the one running the inGRAINED patterns. It's the CAPtain but it's NOT the daily 'crew' of what makes it all happen. In fact, it igNORES you mostly because you SAY you're changing so many times, but don't actually change, so it thinks you don't really MEAN it.

How many times a day do we say to ourselves that we'll give up sugar, or a habit, or start exercising but never follow through?

Your unconscious mind is laying back on the couch sipping a martini going yeah yeah, here we go again.

Another role of your UNconscious mind is to PROVE YOU RIGHT according to what you have deCIDED to believe.

This is why, regardless of affirmations, you STILL believe the UNconsciously running dialogue. For example, if "I'm UNlovable" is ingrained in your UNconscious belief pattern, the affirmation "I'm loveable" will be overridden by the automated UNconscious programming...

So what you DEEP DOWN BELIEVE is

the ONLY evidence your UNconscious mind will let you NOTICE in reality.

These are your 'filters' (meanings applied in the past by you or ancestors) through which you see the world.

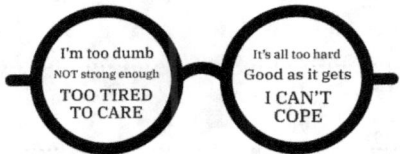

The only way to create a NEW reality is to replace the filters (meanings, these change your beliefs and thoughts).

Remember, for every NEGATIVE filter (belief, value, memory, thought, emotion) there is an opposite.

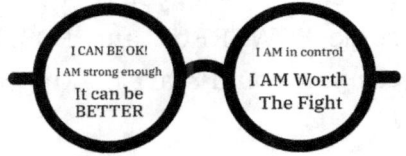

So, the FAStest way to get comPLETE and LASTing change, is to take charge and CHANGE your filters that stop you from moving FORward in life.

CHALLENGE:

Name three (3) people that are in a similar situation to you BUT they DON'T see it through the same lens as YOU!

1 ....

2 ....

3 ....

EXERCISE

What choices are YOU making right now that are keeping you stuck in the pattern / cycle you're in? What are some POWERFUL and POSITIVE choices you could start making right NOW?

Nothing changes if nothing changes.

Remember...

YOU ARE

WORTH **T**HE **F**IGHT!

Have you heard the saying "The definition of insanity is doing the same thing over and over and expecting a different result"?

While you can't change the EVENT that has brought about your emotional and mental pain, YOU CAN change how you see it and therefore DEcrease its ability to TRIGGER you anymore.

Who are you ALREADY a ROLE model to or WILL be to in your lifetime? Kids? Grandkids? Family? Friends? The Community? The underprivileged? The downtrodden? Youth? YOURSELF?

When you see YOURSELF as a ROLE model you bring out the LEADer in you, which is taking control of the power of your CONSCIOUS mind.

By placing yourself as a ROLE MODEL in society you naturally start to take more responsibility for not just yourself, but YOUR effect on OTHERS.

If you are a parent you're a role model MORE than you are a disciplinarian.

Kids do not do what you SAY — they DO what you DO. How THEY handle stress for example is MODELLED not taught.

Don't feel bad if you haven't been the kind of parent you WANT for your kids, it's likely you're running ancestral patterns and you can CHANGE them remember. That's why you're reading this book.

You've done the best you could with your level of knowledge and understanding. From this moment forward though BEGINS A NEW BEGINNING.

The LINK between FEELings and THOUGHTS.

You need to come out of your head and into your body to recognise and learn. Did you know that FEELings are a PHYSICAL thing? We often think that mind-set is something that ONLY affects the brain. Your thoughts BECOME feelings and this creates a looping of thoughts and feelings that gets deeply ingrained the more you do it. Here is a QUICK exercise to demonstrate.

Read through the steps below to understand the exercise THEN close your eyes and actually DO the exercise:

EXERCISE

1. Think about a memory that always causes you to feel negative feelings and then;

2. while you're FEELing that, based on reliving the MEMORY, notice you can FEEEEEEEL it in a SPECIFIC area of your TORso. You'll notice that there's an ACTUAL LOCATION where you FEEEEEEEL it at a specific level of inTENSity. It even has a size and shape to it.

   Many people have never really taken the time to slow down what happens in the moments where we feel down and out, because we're too 'in it'. A bit like childbirth. You don't see the miracle while you're in 15/10 pain.

It's important to note that 'FEELings' IMpact our cells and have the POWER to CAUSE actual muscles to TENSE up or release hormones (chemicals) which flood all eleven of our bodily systems, and pushes adrenaline out to our extremities right to the surface of our skin.

It's interesting that over time we've come to think of our body as a lump of live flesh only, when it actually synchronises WITH our feelings, all triggered through the invisible workings of our MIND.

Not unlike the flourishing of our planet being influenced either positively or negatively by the invisible forces of nature such as oxygen and sun rays.

Our Gut (physical sensations), Heart (feelings) and Mind (brains perceptions) are ALL affected when we're struggling emotionally and mentally. THIS is anOTHER reason to get our sh!t sorted. It's unHEALTHY.

We'll call feelings that stem from our emotions 'charge' felt in your body.

When first applying the MEANING to the trigger event, brain scans show activity at the FRONT part of the brain called the frontal 'lobe'. This is the area of the brain where we make decisions.

At warp speed, once we've interpreted the event (applied 'meaning' to it) as being one of extreme concern, this triggers the FEELING to start in the body at the SAME time as the LIGHTS turn on at the BACK of the brain, an area called the AMYGDALA.

The lights at the FRONT dim according to the inTENSity of the CHARGE, LITERALLY dumbing us down. If the charge is VERY INTENSE, the lights can go out altogether at the front, brightening at the back, causing a stress response as the FEELING becomes entirely physical in the body.

If it's an inHERITed response it may BYPASS the intelligence FRONTAL lobe of our brain entirely, lighting up the BACK of the brain, as we've been epigenetically conditioned to do.

This is meant to keep us safe by putting us into a stress response when at times, UNDER REAL THREAT is a GOOD thing.

EMOTIONAL decisions that get made during this 'stress response' process causes us to react to situations and events in a less than constructive and regrettable way.

We're going to teach you how to turn OFF the emotion 'IN THE MOMENT' so your lights COME BACK ON in the FRONT of your brain and you can make more intelligent decisions 'IN THE MOMENT'. Cool or what!?

"I am separate to my thoughts and feelings, therefore I AM in control of them."

EMOTIONAL RESILIENCE TOOLS

This FIRST TOOL is called BALLOON POPPING.

It's used in-the-moment when feeling negative 'charge' in your body, thus helping you to think straight so you can make better choices, and all done as easily as popping an imaginary balloon!

HOW TO BALLOON POP

Think about whatever you have to think about, a memory that causes you to FEEL (eg. hurt, guilt, sadness, anger etc.) then simply...

Imagine the emotion is the air contained inside a balloon that is INSIDE of you.

Wherever in your body you feel that emotion, imagine that emotion is the air that is within a filled balloon right there.

Now you know what a balloon looks like full and also when it pops? It is just a bit of shrivelled up rubber, right?

NOW, imagine that you hold a big sharp needle and pop that emotion filled balloon, and then ask yourself: 'Now where has the emotion gone?' POP! Just like that, it is gone. Perhaps it ran out your toes and into the gutter down the street?

How incredibly cool is that?!

Tool 2 is called
The 5 Finger Fluster Buster

> It's used Daily to achieve
> Instant Calm as Needed.

ReGARDless of ALL the reasons you already have to RAISE your emotional intelligence and assign better meanings to events that happen in your life, your peace of mind is enough reason alone, ISN'T IT?

Peace and *contentment* are included amongst most people's HIGHEST values. They're usually what we ALL seek, however the ways we go about searching for peace are not usually the ACTUAL way to create a peaceful and contented life.

The 5 Finger Fluster Buster process is a great tool with many benefits, including:

- It helps with Brainstorming.

- It helps us to search for different meanings to situations and can really get our creative juices flowing in us.

- It totally evolves our thinking to a new level of awareness and growth.

- It helps us to uncover new choices, options and ideas.

- It helps us to take charge in the moment and over time, with practice, becomes an automatic response.

NOW, here's how to do the 5 Finger Fluster Buster exercise:

- Step 1 is your thumb = the **TRIGGER** (the event);

- Step 2 is your pointer finger = the **MEANING** (you apply);

- Step 3 is middle finger = the **THOUGHTS** (that follow the meaning);

- Step 4 is your ring finger = the **FEELINGS** (that follow the thoughts);

- Step 5 is your little finger = the **BEHAVIOUR** (that follows the feelings).

Step 2 is where your POWER lies. Notice when pointing that finger your other three fingers are pointing back at YOU — to remind you that it's YOU that assigns the meaning in the FIRST place.

Here's an example:

THE EVENT / TRIGGER: You're driving along and a car pulls out in front of you causing you to slam the brakes on to avoid a collision.

THE MEANING: The meaning you could give that event is likely to be a strong negative one.

👉 THE THOUGHTS: The meaning you have applied causes you to THINK negative thoughts such as "I need my car to get to work every day and it almost got smashed" or worse "I almost got killed" and;

👉 THE FEELINGS: THAT leads you to feel a certain way, probably anything but happy in this instance.

👉 THE BEHAVIOUR: THAT causes you to behave in a way that likely leads to you having an entirely bad day.

An alternative option could have been to apply a DIFFERENT meaning such as "I hope that person wasn't having a heart attack" or "I hope they haven't just had bad news about a family member and now they're rushing to the hospital."

Can you see and feel the difference?

Which meaning will empower **YOU** to have the best and happiest day?

Notice how we tend to UNconsciously bypass the meaning and jump straight into our thoughts, which in turn create the feelings that inevitably lead to the behaviours?

Whenever you find yourself behaving badly or feeling negative, START AGAIN. CONsciously CHANGE the meaning to change your behaviour.

It TEACHES you to become optimistic and before long you have the most valuable habit you could EVER adopt.

MAKE IT A GAME with family and friends. See how MANY options you can come up with for each shitty situation. The LESS you feel like doing it the MORE you NEED to do it.

You have more choices than you realise. Hundreds, if not thousands of choices — BETTER choices that could CHANGE your situation and TURN YOUR LIFE AROUND.

When you claim your POWER TO CHOOSE and give INTENTIONal and emPOWERing MEANING to situations as they arise, life will CHANGE and you're going to become mentally and emotionally much STRONGER, RESILIENT and happier.

"The point where we apply 'meaning' is where our point of personal power lies."

If there are only TWO things you remember about this book I hope it's this message, of course along with THE MANTRA...

"I AM Worth The Fight!"

Tool 3 is called
WORD SWAPPING

This exercise is great for finding out what your inner head-talk is REALLY like and reprogramming it where needed.

You're going to learn how to identify your sabotaging words and rePLACE them with alternatives that will change your inner head-talk.

Check out the following table:

Sabotage Word	Replace With
Should	Will (or want to)
Can't	Can
But	And
Don't	Do
Need	Want
Hate	Love

Sabotage Word	Replace With
Dislike	Like
Always	Never
Sometimes	Often or never
Never	Always or sometimes
Lazy	Energetic
Could	Can
Might	Will
Unworthy	Worthy
Try	Will or want to

Here's how to do it.

Upon first waking up in the morning of a brand new day, 'free write' for 10-15 minutes onto paper whatever thoughts you are thinking. No time to edit, just free write a few pages before you fully wake. Let the thoughts and feelings come out in no particular manner, just let them come. Do this FIRST before anything else. Do it before you climb out of bed and before you have breakfast.

Prepare the night before. Have pen and paper beside your bed so you're all set in the morning.

Once you get started you'll be surprised at just how many thoughts are already running through your head before your day has even started.

Say each of these sentences below out loud and notice the power and purpose in the second sentence of each example where we have completed the 'word swap'.

Say these words out loud AS IF you mean them.

Example 1

"I *never* meet anyone friendly."
"I **ALWAYS** meet friendly people."

Example 2

"I *need* to wash the car."
"I **WANT** to wash the car.

Example 3

"I *should* do that work I *have been putting off.*"
"I **WILL** do that work and I **WANT** to do that work NOW."

Can you think of any of your own examples?

Did you notice the different level of resistance and the different mood and attitude each one creates for you? Notice which ones made you feel empowered.

By changing just a few words in our language we literally change our world. YES! It's that simple.

What about this:

"Honey, you *never* empty the bins" versus "Honey, I **LOVE** it when you empty the bins."

Did you notice the possibility this information implies? Which one will cause least resistance in your partner do you think? Absolutely! Change your words and you CAN transform your relationships.

COMMUNICATION IS KEY, EVEN FROM YOURSELF TO YOURSELF.

An exercise book or notebook is good for this but here's a few pages to use initially. If you already have a journal you may like to use that.

When you've finished your free writing go back and read it over again BUT

THIS TIME, cross out any sabotaging words and WORD SWAP them for an empowering word like the ones we showed you in the above examples. Sometimes you may need to re-write the sentence and other times it will be a straight word swap, one for another.

DAY 1
WORD SWAP JOURNAL

DAY 2
WORD SWAP JOURNAL

DAY 3
WORD SWAP JOURNAL

DAY 4 - WORD SWAP OURNAL

_____
_____
_____
_____
_____
_____
_____
_____
_____
_____
_____
_____
_____
_____
_____
_____
_____
_____
_____
_____
_____
_____

DAY 5 –
WORD SWAP JOURNAL

You MUST put the oxygen mask on yourself, therefore putting yourself FIRST, if you are to have your cup full so that you have something to give others — because YOU are

WORTH THE FIGHT!

I.D.I. ACTIVITIES

We've compiled a list of IDI (I Deserve It) activities that are designed to keep you engaged and supported for the life changing steps that YOU have committed to because YOU decided

"I DESERVE IT"

Each week, indulge in at least three of the activities on the list, checking them off as you complete them. This trains your brain and sends the message to your UNconscious mind that you ARE serious about growing yourself long term.

LIST

Trivia – Learn an interesting or funny fact daily for 3 weeks	
Buy a new item for one of the rooms in your home (eg. coffee mug, ornament, cushion)	
Call an old friend	
Rearrange a room in your home and/or swap something around (eg. position of photos)	
Brush your teeth starting on the opposite side to where you normally would	
Watch a movie or a show that you haven't seen before	
Treat yourself (eg. go out for coffee or dinner)	

Ask yourself this question every day " What is the best thing that has happened to me today?" and then share that positive thing with family or a friend.	
Re-organise your pantry / cupboard and throw out anything that is past its Use By Date	
Watch a 'brains game' video on YouTube	
Start a Pinterest board of something you are interested in	
Make a playlist of upbeat and fun songs- listen to at least one different one each day or listen to all of them	

Have a fun board games night at home with family and / or friends	
Dance like no-one is watching (first thing in the morning is a great way to start the day)	
Take photographs of nature (eg. rainbows, landscapes, sunrises, sunsets etc)	
Make a Vision Board using cut outs from magazines – words and pictures of what you want in the future (eg. new car, holiday etc)	
Get an adult (or a kids) colouring book and new colour pencils and colour a different page each day for 3 weeks	
Take a 20 minute power nap	

Treat yourself to a massage	
Start a gratitude journal and write what you most appreciate and truly be thankful.	

You can add your own fun and new things to the list if you want to.

I'm Not OK

MAINTAINING 'YOU'

Take 1 twice a day

Do an exercise you love to stimulate blood flow	
Do Word Swap Journal writing, swap words and read back	
Do a Meditation or Breathing exercise	
Listen to uplifting, motivational music	
Look yourself in the eyes (into your pupils) in a mirror and tell yourself when you were a child, how fantastic he / she is, because she/he's still in there you know. Say " you are beautiful, smart and can do ANYTHING" and / or whatever you want to remind yourself of.	

> Daydream in high definition, your ULTIMATE vision and purpose. Look at your vision board for inspiration.

Are you off your butt feeling more optimistic now you have some practical TOOLS?

Reread this book EVERY TIME you find yourself slipping, and feel like giving up and need reminding that you are...

WORTH
THE
FIGHT!

Kylie is 36 years old, married, has 4 kids and lives in Brisbane, QLD Australia. She's a REAL person like the rest of us.

I was born into a family of Domestic Violence, drug and alcohol abuse, mental illnesses, dysfunctional and unhealthy relationships. I couldn't talk until I was seven or read and write until nineteen. I was diagnosed with dyslexia and learning disabilities at a young age. I spent most of my primary school years in and out of hospital and when I did go to school I was severely bullied for being "dumb, slow and stupid".

I spent most weekends and holidays at my nana's house. From the age of ten I witnessed my nana self-harm in front of me and I watched her go in and out of the mental health wards. At thirteen I started self-harming. I was suicidal for twenty years and just absolutely hated myself and hated my life. I could not stand living in such a cruel world and living such a horrible life. I would quite often get very tired of the fight to live in a world I didn't understand, where I didn't feel like I fitted in or belonged.

I went on to graduate Year 12 and immediately entered my first serious relationship. This resulted in four years of domestic violence, fighting, cheating, self-harming, in and out of shelters, miscarriages and having a baby in the relationship as well as running for my life.

I then met the man of my dreams but brought all of my emotional baggage with me into the relationship and didn't know what love was or how to handle someone loving me, *so I would push him away. I knew if I didn't want to lose my son and new boyfriend that I had to **work** very hard **on myself** to have any chance of a life with them.*

It was a tough journey and sometimes a very lonely one feeling in despair and like nobody understood me. Every time I hit a bump in the road I would go backwards and always felt that I didn't have the strength to go on and that there was no other way out.

*For a long time I **believed** life was too hard, just unfair, everyone was out to get me and nobody cared.*

I went on to have three more children, two with special needs, one in a wheelchair with Cerebral Palsy and Epilepsy. My son that's in a wheelchair just cried and screamed non-stop for the first five years of his life. Already unable to cope, my sons crying and screaming had me teetering on the edge and I had no idea how to handle it all and had no idea what I was going to do. I thought there was no way out and just couldn't keep going.

*I lost my brother to suicide which on top of everything else sent me completely over the edge. That was it, I couldn't handle it anymore and I just wanted to go and join my brother. I had many attempts over the six months after my brothers suicide until one day I **made a decision** and **commitment** to do whatever it took to save my life because there was no way I wanted to put my husband and children through the excruciating pain and suffering that comes with losing a loved one to suicide.*

For the first time in 32 years I decided W.T.F!

I AM **W**orth **T**he **F**ight!

This decision was unlike the others of my past. Just the decision alone was enough to cause me to view the world differently. Commitment to change, then the commitment to that commitment had to be solid and it was. Decisions like this that are made in stone and not sand bring you the HOW. Prior to the decision the 'how' never showed up. Most people don't realise that about how life works.

Anyway, the tools and people I needed to meet seemed to 'show up' in my life. I did courses and learnt special mind exercises and learnt just the basics about how our brain and emotions work. This clarity helped me to love myself and love life like I never had before. I'm now equipped to handle anything that life throws at me.

(In fact the tools in this book are some of what I used to change my life.)

I had the skills to handle life in a healthy way and was living life to its fullest and contributing to the world in a positive, helpful and healthy way.

Then life threw a curveball, again… but I reacted differently this time.

Nineteen months after I lost my brother to suicide I lost my father to suicide and even though I still grieved, it was totally different to how I grieved previously. I didn't want to join my brother and father this time as I now had the skills and was equipped to get through it all in a healthy way.

I now live an amazing life that I absolutely love. ***I have created*** *a loving, healthy, functional, happy, harmonious, caring and close-knit family like I had only dreamt of when I was a child.*

My focus is no longer on me and my pain and suffering.

I NOW BELIEVE I'M RESILIENT AND THAT LIFE'S NOT A CURSE BUT PERSPECTIVE SURE CAN BE!

*My **whole perspective** on life **has changed** for the better and because I've had a totally* *different **perspective shift** I'm making **better life choices** and experiencing **better results**.*

Now when life gets hard I know I'm fully equipped to handle it and can deal with anything that happens...

Because I decided I AM **W**orth **T**he **F**ight!

Feeling inspired? Turn back to page 38 and continue on.

Paul H is 56 years old, divorced and loves riding his motorcycle. He's a REAL person like the rest of us.

I had a wonderful life. It had panned out just as I had dreamed and I was happy (I thought at the time). I had met the most beautiful woman in the world, we fell in love, eventually married and with our first child we bought a hobby farm in a beautiful spot. We designed and built our dream house that overlooked a large dam and a hill full of giant, ancient trees. We couldn't see another house from our land. By the time our second child came along we were living in the house, had our horses on the property and were breeding llamas. We started a small llama-trekking business and everything was going so well. I envisaged the children growing up on the farm and having a great country life. Everything was perfect.

It's hard to know where it started but things started becoming strained and we seemed to have lost the magic in our relationship. I put it down to just that time of life being very busy with jobs, the farm, two young children. Then the announcement came that she wanted to separate. There was a third person in the mix. She had met someone else and wanted to end what we had created. The dream came crumbling down as we put the farm up for sale, ended the business and started selling the livestock. Finally it sold and I realised I'd pushed all the rest of my life aside and I was totally invested in the marriage and farm. Now it was gone.

I hit the lowest point in my life with the new partner of my wife actively making it difficult to see my kids. I didn't have enough money to buy into a new place because we had borrowed heavily for our lifestyle and came out of it with debt. I felt homeless, alone, abandoned. I became depressed and eventually left my job, not being able to cope with the demands of it as the rest of my life fell apart. I wasn't in the city I had been raised so I had no family or old friend support and I felt like I was in the wilderness, wanting to see my kids when I could and being bound to this place where I no longer wanted to be. I felt trapped with no way out. I couldn't see any way I could be happy again. I had a few short relationships, but always they were unfulfilling. Slowly I started to build my life again and became a weekend father twice a month and I missed being part of my children's lives as they grew.

Travel had always been a big part of my life so eventually when the kids were old enough to understand, I moved to another city, another job, another life. There was still something missing so I started on a journey of self-discovery and studied many self-help books, went to workshops and learnt what it was that made me tick. I really got to know myself, who I was, what I wanted and particularly what I didn't want. At this point anything I didn't want I removed from my life. I had reached the point where I decided W.T.F!

I AM Worth The Fight!

My biggest lesson came as I realised that all the suffering I had going on in my head was the way I was thinking and what I was focusing on. **I started taking responsibility for my life and how I felt.** *I stopped judging other people and **I stopped blaming other people** for my unhappiness and the 'bad' things that had happened in my life. **I became aware of who I was,** what I was saying, and the effect my words and mood were having on other people. I found forgiveness for my ex-wife and her partner... who she only stayed with for a few years anyway. I started seeing that the person I was being at the time was not who I wanted* *to be and eventually could even see where I had not been a good husband, father, man. I even understood why I couldn't keep my marriage together. I had so much to learn about myself and I could now see myself from the outside looking in, as other people saw me.*

My life is wonderful again. *Travel was important to me because it gave me freedom and I now know that freedom is my strongest value. While I was looking for freedom everywhere else, I finally found it inside myself. My life is wonderful because I have freedom in my mind. Freedom to choose, to move, to change, to love who I choose. I also have the freedom to have people in my life that support and enhance my life and remove those from my life that don't... and sometimes that has meant family members. I now realise that the woman I chose to marry was not even the right woman for me and if I knew myself then (as I do now) we probably would have just dated for a couple of months, nothing more.*

I often get told I am the happiest person people have met. I don't buy into people's dramas... including the world of politics... and live my life focusing on being happy with who I am today, now, in this very moment. I've found myself living on another small farm surrounded by people who support and love me. I travel regularly and now have three grandchildren, while the relationship with my own children continues to grow stronger every day.

I thought I had a wonderful life before, but back then I still didn't really understand the full meaning of wonderful. Today my life is truly wonderful...

Because I decided I AM **W**orth **T**he **F**ight!

Feeling inspired? Turn back to page 38 and continue on.

Hannah is 24 and engaged to be married. She's a REAL person like the rest of us.

Hi I'm Hannah and I started struggling with my mental health when I was 12 and suffered with depression, anxiety and an eating disorder for a little over 10 years. At school I always felt the odd one out. I was very isolated and struggled to make friends.

After school, aged 17 I tried running from my challenges and travelled to Europe for 7 months. I had an amazing time and got to know our family in Germany really well. But my problems followed me.

When I got home I moved out and started University and this is when things started to go really downhill. The eating disorder spiralled out of control, I was self-harming and within a year I was hospitalized and spent 4 months on an eating disorder program where I gained weight but that just meant constant screaming in my head from the eating disorder part of me and the depression, anxiety and self-harm got way worse.

When I reached my goal weight I was discharged. However hospital had become such a crutch and I was around people who got me and I could hide from the rest of the world and I didn't cope with going home. After only two days at home I attempted suicide for the first time and landed straight back in hospital.

After that I spent almost the entirety of two years in hospital. I was trialled on every single antidepressant without any effect. I had multiple rounds of ECT (electroconvulsive therapy) which only caused short term memory loss and no real reprieve. All the time I was still finding ways to self-harm, even though I was under very close watch from nurses. I attempted suicide twice more during that two years and I genuinely believed (and hoped) that I would not make it to my 21st birthday.

I just wanted the suffering to end. I was done with trying to get better and not getting anywhere, just going around and around in circles.

One day I realised the harder I tried to get better, the more I focussed on my illness and the worse it got. So I decided to stop trying so hard and instead of focussing on my struggles and instead of worrying when I slipped up, I just started learning to relax and to focus on life outside of hospital. One thing I did know at this point was I had decided W.T.F!

I AM **W**orth **T**he **F**ight!

I began a Yoga teacher training which for me saved my life and I slowly began to learn how to feel safe in my body and to regulate my emotions in effective ways. It was really hard. And to stop trying so hard to get better was counter intuitive because I thought that if I stopped trying I would never get better. But I soon realised the more I let go the more the negative behaviours and emotions just fell away.

Now I consider myself fully recovered. I am happy and healthy. I love life. I've met a beautiful man and we are getting married next year. I'm brewing beer and making wine for a living (in the family business). I'm teaching Yoga and studying Counselling. And I am so, so, so grateful that I didn't end my life. I have come so far. I have tools to get through the tough times without relapsing and spiralling back into the void. I feel relaxed and comfortable in my body. I can see the joy in life instead of only seeing darkness. It's been a tough journey climbing out of the pits of mental illness but I have made it and I'm grateful for the person I am thanks to the experiences I've had...

Because I decided I AM **W**orth **T**he **F**ight!

Feeling inspired? Turn back to page 38 and continue on.

Jaimie is 17 years old, lives on the Gold Coast and is following her dreams of becoming a professional dancer. She's a REAL person like the rest of us.

I remember when I was a young child I felt like I didn't have a care in the world. I loved going to school and I made friends easily. I knew from the early age of 4, when I first started Kindergarten, I was going to travel the world performing to make people smile.

My parents separated when I was 6 years old and while I predominantly lived with my mum and step-dad I spent regular weekend and holiday time with my dad. A few years later dad found a new partner and I now had two homes and two sets of parents. Mum and dad got on pretty well so it felt like I had one big family.

My school life had been nothing short of a fun experience. During the last couple of years at Primary school I had even been lucky enough to travel overseas twice with my mum and step dad and I'd taken a road trip from our home in NSW to Far North QLD with my dad, grandad and older brother. I graduated from Year 6 feeling on top of the world. I simply loved life and couldn't wait to get to high school.

I was only 11 when I started high school, a year younger than a lot of the kids in my year. I loved high school. I was doing well academically, was a member of the Student Representative Council, played in every single sports team (including girls footy) and participated in music and drama performances. Outside of school I participated in Physical Culture which was a year-round commitment. I had been doing Physi since I was 7.

Up until this point I didn't have a care in the world. I loved school. I had plenty of friends. I had two loving homes and my parents and step-parents all supported and encouraged me to follow my dreams. I was the most confident kid I knew.

In December that year my dad had a heart attack. Turns out the doctors established he'd most likely been having heart attacks for several years. He was rushed to St Vincent's hospital by Air Ambulance and had double bypass surgery. I travelled to Sydney to be by his side – I couldn't bear not to be with him.

We returned home a few days later. I was relieved he was out of the hospital and glad to be home but that didn't last long. My dad collapsed and had a cardiac arrest in front of me. It was then that my whole world fell apart...

My dad died but the Paramedics revived him on the way to hospital. They saved his life! Dad was sent back to St Vincent's. He suffered another two cardiac arrests while in the hospital and was eventually discharged after undergoing surgery to fit him with an internal defibrillator.

Even though my dad had survived my life spiralled downwards. I became anxious and fearful. I couldn't relax. I was hyper-sensitive and hyper-vigilant. I was triggered on an almost daily basis and school had become hell on earth. I struggled to maintain friendships and for the first time in my life I felt lost and alone.

I was diagnosed with Anxiety and Post Traumatic Stress Disorder. I started seeing a counsellor but the more I went to counselling the more hopeless and helpless I felt. Talking about what happened wasn't making me better, it was making me worse and I was dizzy from going around in circles. I knew I needed to get the focus off what had happened and back onto what I wanted to do with my life I decided W.T.F!.

I AM **W**orth **T**he **F**ight!

I changed schools and made new friends. I joined a local Youth Group. I started dancing and found my passion. Even on my darkest days dancing was something I had to look forward to. If I was dancing, I was breathing. I started to remember who the confident kid who didn't have a care in the world was and I liked it.

I spent six days a week dancing and started teaching classes in my down time. I even travelled to America and danced onstage at Disneyland and in their Summer Parade.

Earlier this year I relocated to the Gold Coast, leaving my family behind in NSW, to commence a part-time dance course. I'm dancing with one of the most prestigious

Performing Arts studios on the East Coast. In 2019 I will be dancing full-time and a step closer to fulfilling my dream of becoming a professional dancer.

Looking back I can see how the point in time where I shifted my FOCUS was the point I broke through the pain and suffering. Today I'm grateful to be LIVING life to the FULLEST...

Because I decided I AM **W**orth **T**he **F**ight!

Feeling inspired? Turn back to page 38 and continue on.

Paul S. is 39 years old and has a background in construction, particularly in the FIFO (Fly In Fly Out) industry. He's a REAL person like the rest of us.

At 22 my whole world changed. Life was good. I was building houses working the very job I'd always wanted. I had met a woman with a 15 month old son and things progressed very quickly between us and we were married within 6 months. I went from being a boy to married man, becoming a father figure all while hiding a drug habit behind the scenes. I was a functioning addict, with bills to pay and mouths to feed... and then we had a daughter.

Life was tough behind the scenes although the facade looked like the perfect life. After years of verbal anger and high tensions we separated and fought it out in court for access rights. Things started to change and I broke my drug habit and reskilled. After three years apart we got back together. I thought we had changed and that we could make it work, but things began to spiral out of control again very quickly.

I chased what I thought I needed, what my kids needed, but the volatile relationship again took hold. I had created a world of lies and arguments that led to severe anxiety and depression and heavy drinking. I knew something had to change and the final straw led to divorce, which saw me completely hide away from society and the mess I was in. I struggled to face the public, the friends I had lost, the family I had chosen against and the person I had become.

I buried myself in work and began in the FIFO industry to escape the reality

I was in. I managed to structure rosters as best as possible for the kids so I could slowly rebuild my life. Construction again became my priority and by this stage I was supervising large crews and running large projects, but the stress began to creep in and the anger began to resurface and the negative thoughts began to take hold.

Was I good enough, did I deserve my position, was I worth it? I bottled it up and hid it away knowing I was doing it for the kids. I had become a slave to the job and too frightened to walk away from the money. Project after project I chased the position, the salary, the lifestyle I thought I was creating. Then the kids moved away and my world changed again.

I had nothing to keep me where I was. The house I was renovating after long hours at work... a limited social life and the loneliness of being single where all just reminders of where I had failed. I felt lost, scared and embarrassed at who I had become. I felt like a failure and believed I was doomed to grow to be a lonely old man. Then life turned again. I was offered an overseas position and a ray of hope.

Going to a country I knew nothing about in an area of the Middle East created much excitement, fear and anxiety all rolled in together. From the moment I stepped on the plane my world would never be the same. Buried in work from the moment I arrived and the stress of a new culture, a language barrier, the responsibility and the expectation I felt like I'd jumped out of the fire and into the frying pan.

I became a recluse and would hide in my room. Some days I would hide from work, making excuses as to why I couldn't be there. I battled myself through fear of others perceptions of me. I knew I could do more for myself but I didn't know what or how. It was such an ironic feeling knowing I was the one in charge of hundreds of men and their safety. I could see it in them yet I couldn't admit it in me. Not being able to take much more I knew something or someone had to give and that someone was me. I finally decided W.T.F!

I AM **W**orth **T**he **F**ight!

I started to exercise and look after myself. I engaged in sport and began to read and listen to audio books. I shifted my routine and took on personal coaches to help keep me accountable and focused on completing my contract as honouring that commitment was important to me.

I began to see change and it gave me focus to continue. At times I would feel I was getting on top, but then those old feelings would creep back in and I'd be back to square one. I often wondered to myself just how many times would I have to go through this before I gave up? I felt like I was so close to beating it and I couldn't give in knowing that not only my kids needed me, but I needed me too. I never gave up although eventually I realised the FIFO industry wasn't for me.

I look back and am so grateful for the fight. The lowest times taught me so much and today with the tools I have learnt since then I am alive again in spirit and mind. I feel like a new man. I have an amazing new partner and a new family. My kids are so happy to have their dad home and not so cranky or stressed out. I have a smile on my face every day knowing how lucky I am to be here and to be able to share my story with other men.

You see, I used think it was "tough" to be able to bottle it up and get on with things but what I've since learnt and wholeheartedly know, is that it takes a bigger man to own it, want more and do something about it. I turned my life around...

Because I decided I AM **W**orth **T**he **F**ight!

Turn back to page 38 and continue on.

For anyone ELSE you know who needs reminding they are WORTH THE FIGHT, pay it forward now and support the charity RISE ABOVE IT's programs and resource development at the same time.

Go to www.riseaboveit.org.au and order copies to gift forward and have on hand for when you ask "R U OK?" And they say "NO, I'M NOT".

TOGETHER we can BREAK THE CYCLE.

The author's mission is to set 10 MILLION HEARTS FREE. To see other ways you could get involved, go to www.mazschirmer.com.au

Remember

YOU are W. T. F!

(**W**orth **T**he **F**ight)

HELPLINE SERVICES
(Australia Only)

If you're having suicidal thoughts please call 000. Otherwise contact one of these services:

Lifeline
Phone: 13 11 14
www.lifeline.org.au

Suicide Call Back Service
Phone: 1300 659 467
www.suicidecallbackservice.org.au

Kids Helpline
Phone: 1800 55 1800
www.kidshelp.com.au

MensLine Australia
Phone: 1300 78 99 78
www.mensline.org.au

For Domestic or Family Abuse
Phone: 1800 73 77 32
www.1800respect.org.au
NRS: 1800 55 56 77
Interpreter: 13 14 50

WTF Do I Do Now?

I'm Not OK

www.ingramcontent.com/pod-product-compliance
Lightning Source LLC
Chambersburg PA
CBHW072049290426
44110CB00014B/1606